NATIONAL AERONAUTICS AND SPACE ADMINISTRATION

AGENTS OF GOVERNMENT

TERESA WIMMER

Creative Education · Creative Paperbacks

Published by Creative Education and Creative Paperbacks
P.O. Box 227, Mankato, Minnesota 56002
Creative Education and Creative Paperbacks are
imprints of The Creative Company
www.thecreativecompany.us

Design and production by Chelsey Luther
Art direction by Rita Marshall

Printed in Malaysia

Photographs by Alamy (NASA Archive, NASA Collection, NG Images, RIA Novosti), Corbis
(Bettmann, Ben Cooper/Science Faction, Corbis, Steven Hobbs/Stocktrek Images, NASA,
NASA – digital version copyright/Science Faction, Cheryl Power/Science Photo Library,
Boris Roessler/dpa), deviantART (AllydNYC), Defense Video & Imagery Distribution
System (NASA), Flickr (NASA, NASA/Bill Ingalls), Getty Images (Albert Klein, NASA –
Apollo/digital version by Science Faction), HubbleSite (NASA/ESA/M. Livio and the Hubble
20th Anniversary Team [STScI]), NASA (ESA/NASA, NASA, NASA/MSFC, NASA/ESA/
Hubble SM4 ERO Team), Shutterstock (leonello calvetti)

Library of Congress Cataloging-in-Publication Data
Wimmer, Teresa.
National Aeronautics and Space Administration / Teresa Wimmer.
p. cm. — (Agents of government)
Summary: An in-depth look at the people and policies behind the government agency known
as NASA, from its founding in 1958 to the controversies and challenges it faces today.
Includes bibliographical references and index.

ISBN 978-1-60818-547-4 (hardcover)
ISBN 978-1-62832-148-7 (pbk)
1. United States. National Aeronautics and Space Administration—Juvenile literature. 2.
United States. National Aeronautics and Space Administration—History—Juvenile literature.
3. Astronautics—United States—Juvenile literature. 4. Outer space—Exploration—United
States—Juvenile literature. 5. Outer space—Exploration—History—Juvenile literature. I. Title.

TL789.8.U5W56 2015
629.4'0973—dc23   2014029607

CCSS: RI.5.1, 2, 3, 5, 6, 8; RH.6-8.3, 4, 5, 8

First Edition HC 9 8 7 6 5 4 3 2 1
First Edition PBK 9 8 7 6 5 4 3 2 1

TABLE OF CONTENTS

Since its founding in 1958, the National Aeronautics and Space Administration (NASA) has become a world leader in space exploration,

discovery, and travel. Spurred on by competition with the Soviet Union, the United States realized it needed an agency solely dedicated to developing space technology and overseeing its space efforts. NASA was thus created to "plan, direct, and conduct aeronautical and space activities." In a special message to the U.S. Congress on May 25, 1961, president John F. Kennedy said, "Now it is time to take longer strides—time for a great new American enterprise—time for this nation to take a clearly leading role in space achievement, which in many ways may hold the key to our future on Earth." NASA would indeed be the key to unlocking that mysterious "enterprise" in the decades that followed. Without it, people may not know what Mars looks like or how it is possible to conduct experiments in a space station. Although its path has not always been smooth, NASA continues to pursue its vision, reaching toward new heights and revealing the unknown so that what it does and learns will benefit all humankind.

NASA's long-running space shuttle program came to define the agency and make it visible to everyday Americans.

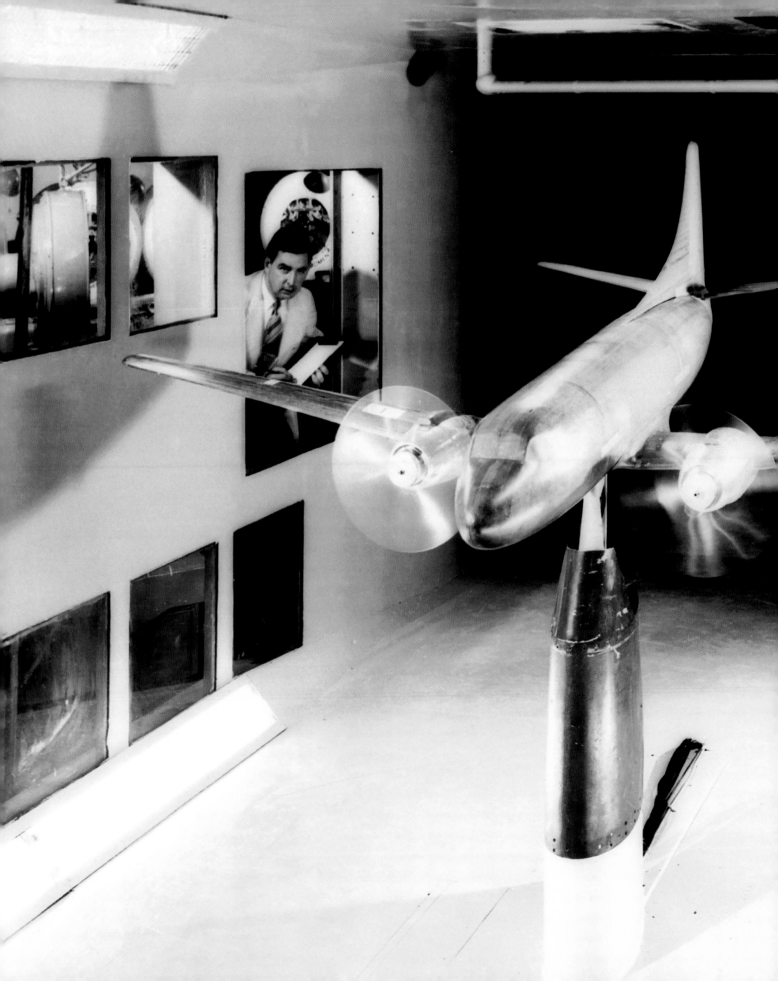

Space Race

Before Congress and the president created
NASA in 1958, an organization called the
National Advisory Committee for Aeronautics
(NACA) led the country's efforts in the skies.
NACA was established in 1915 as a cooperative
effort among industry, universities, the military,
and the federal government. The early years
of **aviation** involved many accidents. Despite
its small staff of 12 volunteers and budget of
only $5,000, NACA embarked on a mission to
research flight problems and devise solutions
to help aviation progress. By the 1920s, NACA
had developed an impressive collection of in-
house wind tunnels, engine test stands, and
flight test facilities.

In the 1930s, NACA scientists encouraged to
pursue their own research developed such breakthroughs as **airfoil** and **cowling** technology,
which allowed aircraft to be more streamlined
and to use less fuel. NACA also was responsible
for designing the first aircraft to break the sound
barrier. On October 14, 1947, U.S. Air Force
Captain Chuck Yeager lifted off from Muroc
Army Air Field (now Edwards Air Force Base) in

*Wind tunnels in such
testing sites as Langley
Research Center were
inherited from NACA–
established facilities.*

California and flew the *X-1* research plane faster than the speed of sound.

After World War II, the U.S. and Soviet Union entered the **Cold War**. During this period, space exploration emerged as a major area of competition between the two nations. From 1955 to 1972, the Space Race was on. After U.S. president Dwight D. Eisenhower approved a plan to put a data-gathering satellite in **Earth orbit** by December 31, 1958, the Soviets announced their intention to launch a satellite, too.

History was made on October 4, 1957, when the Soviet Union reached space before the U.S. by successfully launching *Sputnik I*, the world's first artificial satellite. Americans feared that this satellite meant that the capability of launching ballistic missiles carrying **nuclear** weapons was not far behind. *Sputnik* also signaled a technological gap between the U.S. and the Soviet Union, and it prompted Americans to call for more money to be spent on efforts to reach space. Programs were organized to educate people about technical and scientific advancements, and new federal agencies were established to manage air and space research and development. Texas senator Lyndon B. Johnson made a speech to Congress two weeks after the *Sputnik* launch. In it, he called for a congressional review of the American space effort. Johnson believed it was critical that the U.S. should focus new energy on developing its space exploration efforts both to advance technology and to help the U.S. become a leader in the Space Race.

In just three months, the U.S. responded to *Sputnik* by launching its first satellite, *Explorer I*. On January 31, 1958, *Explorer* began orbiting Earth. The scientific instruments on board the satellite soon gave evidence of **radiation** belts encircling the planet. Plans were already underway to launch more satellites. Congress decided that any long-term exploratory projects should probably be handled by a single independent agency.

On July 29, 1958, the National Aeronautics and Space Act combined NACA with other government agencies to create NASA, which officially began operations on October 1. NASA's mission was to expand "human knowledge of

In just three months, the U.S. responded to Sputnik *by launching … Explorer I.*

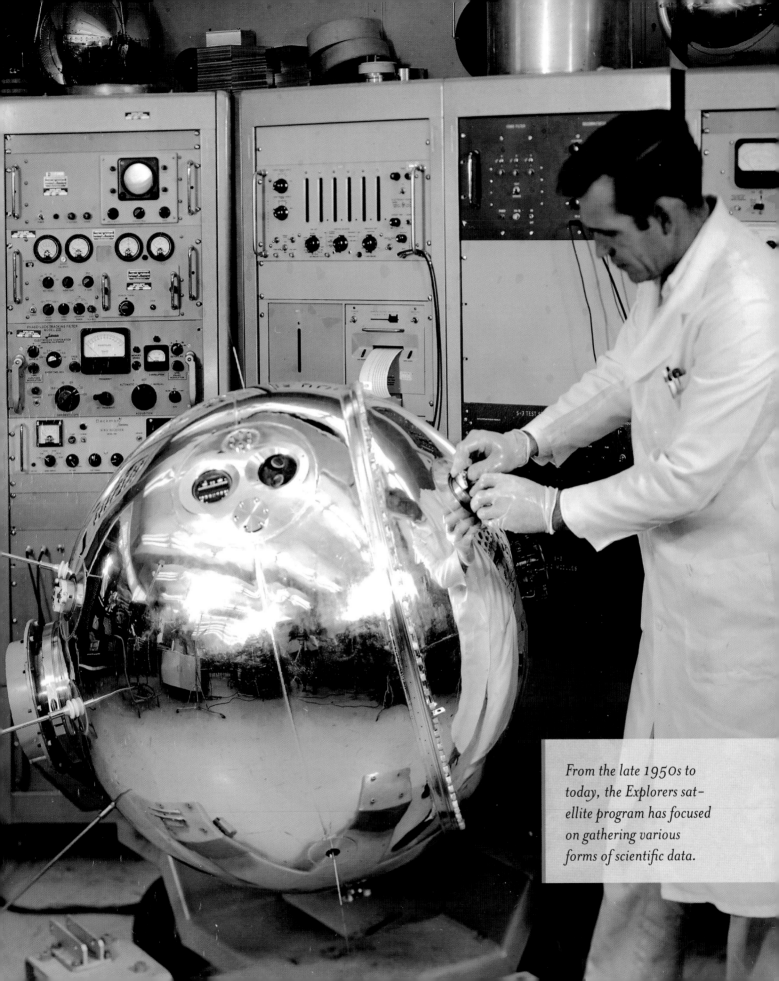

From the late 1950s to today, the Explorers satellite program has focused on gathering various forms of scientific data.

President Kennedy went before Congress to urge the lawmakers to provide funding for his "national goals" in space.

phenomena in the atmosphere and space" and to establish the U.S. "as a leader in aeronautical and space science and technology." Unlike NACA, NASA was created as a civilian agency. Its advancements in space science would be used for peaceful rather than militaristic purposes. Politicians hoped NASA would be a tool for convincing other nations to follow in America's—not the Soviet Union's—footsteps. The U.S. military would also continue supporting space research, especially as NASA became its source for activities such as many satellite and manned aircraft **reconnaissance** missions.

Even before it was formally organized, NASA began proving its worth. Scientists conducted several satellite programs that gathered information about the solar system. They also provided weather and communications services to the American people. Driven by a desire to achieve, NASA expanded rapidly in its first two years. However, it experienced serious growing pains. Many times, rockets that were supposed to boost satellites into orbit did not perform properly. In 1958, only 5 out of 17 satellite launch

attempts were successful, and in 1959, only 10 of 21 satellites made it into orbit. Between 1958 and 1965, though, the U.S. went from a launch failure rate of 71 percent to a launch success rate of 91 percent. Both the U.S. and Soviet Union next set their sights on a more distant frontier: the moon. In October 1958, satellites went up to collect lunar data, but the Soviets' *Luna 2* (launched the following September) was the first to relay images of the moon's surface back to Earth.

In response to the success of *Luna 2*, NASA launched *Ranger 1* on August 23, 1961, but it failed to reach lunar orbit. Compared with the Soviets, NASA's space program still seemed to lag behind. In an attempt to inspire confidence and secure funding for the fledgling agency, President Kennedy had asked the nation in May to "commit itself to achieving the goal, before this decade is out, of landing a man on the moon and returning him safely to the Earth." It was one thing to put an unmanned object into space, but it was another to claim bragging rights on getting a *person* to the moon. However,

Between 1958 and 1965, ... the U.S. went from a launch failure rate of 71 percent to a launch success rate of 91 percent.

both the American people and NASA were invigorated by the challenge put forth by Kennedy.

To fund the moon program, Congress almost doubled NASA's budget between 1961 and 1962, and hundreds of scientists and technical experts were rounded up from America's finest colleges and research centers. At first, these consultants were not pleased with NASA's control over all aspects of spaceflight science. Any experiments requiring the flight of a **payload** first had to meet NASA's guidelines. And all projects fell under the careful eye of NASA officials. A partnership soon developed among all concerned, though, and people from various industries and branches of science began to work together to achieve NASA's space goals.

Project Mercury produced the first success of this newfound partnership. Since 1958, the goal of Project Mercury had been to send a manned spacecraft into Earth orbit and to bring the craft safely back to Earth. On May 5, 1961, U.S. astronaut Alan Shepard, aboard the Mercury *Freedom 7* spacecraft, became the first American in space. (Soviet cosmonaut Yuri Gagarin had been the first person to reach space on April 12, 1961.) Then, on February 20, 1962, astronaut John Glenn became the first American to orbit Earth, circling the planet

AGENCY INSIDER

APOLLO-SOYUZ TEST PROJECT

The first international partnership in space was the Apollo-Soyuz Test Project. On July 17, 1975, an Apollo spacecraft with a crew of three docked with a Soviet Soyuz and its crew of two. The nine-day Apollo-Soyuz mission brought together former spaceflight rivals the U.S. and the Soviet Union. During nearly two days of joint activities, the mission's Soviet cosmonauts and U.S. astronauts carried out five joint experiments. The successful Apollo-Soyuz Test Project paved the way for future international partnerships.

Early computer technology enabled NASA scientists to simulate future spaceflight missions mathematically.

three times aboard *Friendship 7*. Glenn became world-famous, and his Earth orbit was a big boost for Americans' national pride.

Even though all the Mercury flights between 1962 and 1963 were successful, the technology needed to make the leap from human space-flight to landing on the moon was significant. NASA had some big questions to answer: How would the astronauts be able to work outside the spacecraft once it touched down on the moon's surface? How would a craft locate, drive toward, and meet up with another spacecraft in order to return to Earth? To address these questions, NASA laid the groundwork for Project Apollo in May 1961 and, in preparation, began Project Gemini in January 1962. There would be no turning back now.

The work of Mercury astronauts such as Shepard (left) and Glenn (right) paved the way for Projects Gemini and Apollo.

MARS ONE
Netherlands; Destination: Mars

In April 2013, the Dutch company Mars One announced a selection program to send 24 individuals to start a permanent human settlement on Mars. Because the technology to return them to Earth does not exist, the volunteers would live on Mars for the rest of their lives. Mars One contracted with Lockheed Martin and Surrey Satellite Technology Ltd. to build a vehicle for an unmanned mission to the planet in 2018. If that mission is successful, the first pioneers could land on Mars in 2025.

The Final Frontier

Project Gemini was designed to test a two-man spacecraft, record the effects of weightlessness on astronauts during long flights, develop ways of docking with other orbiting vehicles, and perfect methods of reentry into Earth's atmosphere. In June 1965, American astronaut Edward White II, a member of Gemini 4, performed the first American extravehicular activity (spacewalk). The 12 Gemini flights allowed NASA scientists to conduct 52 different experiments and gain necessary technical knowledge about how to land a spacecraft and how to support a human outside the spacecraft.

After Gemini, Apollo—named after the Greek god of poetry, music, and archery—revolutionized NASA by giving it the single goal of putting a human on the moon by the end of the decade. Along with the extra brainpower provided by the legion of scientists, researchers, and technicians now working for NASA, Congress also authorized billions of dollars in additional funding by 1965.

In addition to the work that continued on Apollo, the Lunar Orbiter program helped complete a map of the lunar surface in 1966 and

Ed White used a gas gun to propel himself out of the spacecraft and then pulled on the 26.2-foot (8 m) tether to "walk."

1967. Next, to test how to soft-land a vehicle on the moon, NASA launched the probe *Surveyor 1*, which successfully landed on June 2, 1966. It transmitted more than 10,000 high-quality images of the moon's surface. Finally, on July 16, 1969, the Apollo 11 mission began, with astronauts Neil Armstrong, Edwin "Buzz" Aldrin, and Michael Collins aboard the *Columbia* command **module**. Armstrong became the first man to walk on the moon four days later, proudly proclaiming, "That's one small step for [a] man, one giant leap for mankind." All three astronauts returned to Earth as heroes, and no longer were humans confined to Earth alone.

Even though the Apollo 11 astronauts were idolized by Americans and the rest of the world, some had lost interest in sending anyone else to the moon. The U.S. in 1969 was a very different place than it had been just eight years before. Faced with the Vietnam War crisis, poverty, and race riots in major U.S. cities, many Americans argued that federal funds should be spent on addressing those issues rather than on space travel. Members of the **counterculture** spoke out against the use of science and technology in modern society, seeking a return to a simpler lifestyle. As public support for NASA's programs began to wane, so did its federal funding. The final Apollo mission, Apollo 17, returned from the moon on December 19, 1972.

During the 1970s, NASA fought to hold on to its top scientists and resources with a budget that was only half of what it had been during the Apollo years. However, NASA did enjoy some important accomplishments during this time. It used some of the Apollo technology to create Skylab, the U.S.'s first experimental space station. The 100-ton (90.7 t) orbital workshop was launched May 14, 1973. Two weeks later, the first three astronauts to crew the station arrived. In all, 9 astronauts occupied the Skylab workshop for 171 days and conducted more than 300 experiments in solar astronomy, Earth resources, and medical studies.

As public support for NASA's programs began to wane, so did its federal funding.

Since the 1950s, Americans had been fascinated with the possibility of finding life on Mars, and in the '70s, NASA was finally able to investigate the proposition. The satellite *Viking 2* was launched on September 9, 1975, and landed on Mars one year later. For the next four years, *Viking 2* transmitted data about Mars back to Earth. NASA scientists learned that Mars was too dry and cold to be able to support

Starting with Apollo 11, each U.S. crew to land on the moon planted a flag— most of which still stood, decades later.

The 1986 Challenger explosion stunned the agency and the country, reminding everyone of the risks of spaceflight.

life but did not rule out the possibility that forms of life could have existed thousands of years ago. Americans also got their first glimpse of the outer planets when the *Voyager 1* and *2* probes were launched in the fall of 1977. After their planetary missions ended, both crafts continued exploring the farthest reaches of our solar system. In 2013, NASA announced that *Voyager 1* had entered interstellar space—the space between stars.

As early as the mid-1960s, NASA had envisioned a space shuttle that would frequently transport humans to a space station. On April 12, 1981, NASA saw its dream realized when it launched the space shuttle *Columbia* from Cape Canaveral, Florida. *Columbia* spent two days in space before returning safely to Earth, and the media hailed it as the beginning of a new era in spaceflight. At the time, people thought they would soon be traveling into space as easily as they could drive a car.

The space shuttle program was also important because the shuttle was designed to carry Spacelab—a reusable laboratory. Spacelab allowed scientists to perform experiments in **microgravity** while in orbit. The laboratory comprised many parts, including a pressurized module, an unpressurized carrier, and other related hardware housed in the shuttle's cargo bay. Spacelab components flew on 24 shuttle missions between November 1983 and April 1998. Between 1981 and 1991, 204 people flew on the space shuttle—some more than once.

Then, on January 28, 1986, the unthinkable happened. The space shuttle *Challenger* exploded only 73 seconds after liftoff from Cape Canaveral. All seven crew members were killed, including Christa McAuliffe, who would have been the first civilian in space. An investigation blamed the *Challenger* disaster on faulty **O-rings**, which could not maintain their tight seal in the bitterly cold air. The shuttle program was suspended while NASA's management system was overhauled and confidence could be restored. NASA redesigned its solid rocket boosters, implemented new safety measures, and reworked shuttle components. It also made organizational changes to improve its efficiency and reliability. The "Return to Flight" mission

---

At the time, people thought they would soon be traveling into space as easily as they could drive a car.

---

occurred September 29, 1988, with the launch of the *Discovery* shuttle.

The shuttle of the 1990s carried aboard another revolutionary space technology called the Hubble Space Telescope (HST). Built by NASA, along with contributions from the European Space Agency (ESA), the HST was supposed to have launched in 1986. Not until April 1990 was it carried aboard *Discovery*, though, to take photos of Earth and other space matter. Between 1990 and 2014, Hubble circled Earth more than 110,000 times and snapped more than 570,000 images of 30,000 **celestial** objects. Although not the first space telescope, Hubble was the largest and most versatile and the only telescope designed to be serviced in space by astronauts. Between 1993 and 2009, five shuttle missions repaired, upgraded, and replaced systems on the telescope. The telescope is now expected to function until 2020 and will be succeeded by the James Webb Space Telescope (JWST), scheduled to launch in 2018.

The launch of the International Space Station (ISS) in 1998 marked an unprecedented cooperative effort involving NASA and other international agencies. In 1993, with the Soviet Union disbanded and Cold War ended, the U.S. merged its Freedom space station with Russia's

AGENCY INSIDER

COLUMBIA DISASTER

Unfortunately, the space shuttle *Challenger* disaster was not NASA's only shuttle accident. On February 1, 2003, the space shuttle *Columbia* disintegrated as it returned to Earth, killing all seven astronauts on board. NASA suspended space shuttle flights for more than two years as it investigated the disaster. The cause? A hole on the wing had let in gases that destabilized the pressure inside *Columbia*. It could not withstand the fiery re-entry. The need for a new spaceflight vehicle became painfully obvious.

A new camera installed on the HST in 2009 enabled the telescope to see more areas of star formation in the galaxy.

Mir-2. This eventually led to the creation of the ISS. The cooperative project among the space agencies of the U.S., Russia, Canada, Japan, and Europe serves as a space environment research laboratory. Crew members conduct experiments in biology, physics, astronomy, meteorology, and other fields. They also test spacecraft systems and equipment required for missions to the moon and Mars. Although small, unmanned spacecraft can provide platforms for zero gravity and exposure to space, decades-long studies can be performed in space stations.

Since the arrival of ISS Expedition 1 on November 2, 2000, the ISS has been continuously staffed with a crew of six. After the U.S. shuttle program ended in 2011, NASA relied on Russia to ferry all crew members to the ISS until 2015, when such American companies as Boeing and SpaceX were expected to take over. Spaceflyer Koichi Wakata became the first Japanese person to command the ISS when he took charge of Expedition 39 in March 2014. The ISS is projected to remain in use until at least 2024.

Non-shuttle craft that fly to the ISS in the future will need special adapters to be able to dock with the station.

EUROPEAN SPACE AGENCY
Paris, France

In 2015, the European Space Agency (ESA) celebrated 40 years of space exploration. The ESA was founded in 1975 when the European Launcher Development Organization and the European Space Research Organization merged. Famed for its Giotto space probe, which allowed scientists to examine the core of Halley's Comet in 1986, the agency also collaborates with international partners on projects such as the ISS. The ESA's headquarters are in Paris, France, and it is currently made up of 20 member nations.

Mission Control

From the very beginning, NASA was tasked with developing and overseeing the U.S. space program. As its duties and goals have changed, so have its size and structure. When President Eisenhower created NASA, he appointed an administrator to head the agency. (A 17-member advisory board was also created, but the board had no administrative responsibility.) NASA's first administrator was T. Keith Glennan, and from then on, each NASA administrator has been appointed by the president. In 1958, Eisenhower wanted the NASA administrator to report directly to him, but Senator Johnson (Eisenhower's chief political opponent) did not want NASA to be chaired by the president. Instead, Johnson wanted it to be led by a committee that had the power to solve conflicts and to make sure all members of NASA were working together.

As a compromise, Johnson added the National Aeronautics and Space Council (NASC) to the National Aeronautics and Space Act of 1958. This council consisted of no more than nine members and served as an adviser to NASA. Chaired by the president, the NASC included the

Glennan showed Senator Johnson the flexible Mylar coating that would be used on the inflatable satellite Echo in 1960.

secretaries of state and defense, the NASA administrator, the chairman of the Atomic Energy Commission, and four members chosen by the president. In 1989, the NASC morphed into the National Space Council (NSC). However, tension arose between the astronaut-based management at NASA and the politically motivated NSC. As a result, the NSC was dissolved in 1993, and the National Science and Technology Council (NSTC) took over its functions.

NASA is an independent federal agency responsible for driving "advances in science, technology, and exploration to enhance knowledge, education, innovation, economic vitality, and stewardship of Earth." This includes planning long-term civilian and military aerospace research, launching manned and unmanned missions into space, and training astronauts. NASA is headquartered in Washington, D.C., but many of its employees based in 10 field centers and other facilities around the country carry out the organization's day-to-day operations.

NASA is also advised by two groups, the NASA Advisory Council (NAC) and the Aerospace Safety Advisory Panel (ASAP). NAC is an independent group of scientists and aerospace experts that provides guidance to NASA's senior leadership on ever-changing technical challenges and solutions facing the agency. Established in 1968, ASAP is an independent group of transportation safety experts who evaluate NASA's safety performance and advise the agency on how it can improve. Congress requires ASAP to submit an annual report to NASA's administrator and Congress that describes the safety measures taken by NASA to help prevent mission accidents.

NASA's headquarters is organized into four main organizations called Mission Directorates: Aeronautics Research, Human Exploration and Operations, Science, and Space Technology. The Aeronautics Research directorate develops new flight technologies that help us explore Earth, space, and the universe. Human Exploration and Operations manages work relating to the ISS and other exploratory programs. Science studies Earth and the universe beyond. Space Technology focuses on staying on the cutting edge of new technologies and innovation.

When it began operations in 1958, NASA inherited three primary research laboratories from NACA: Langley Aeronautical Laboratory

> *NASA's headquarters is organized into four main organizations called Mission Directorates ...*

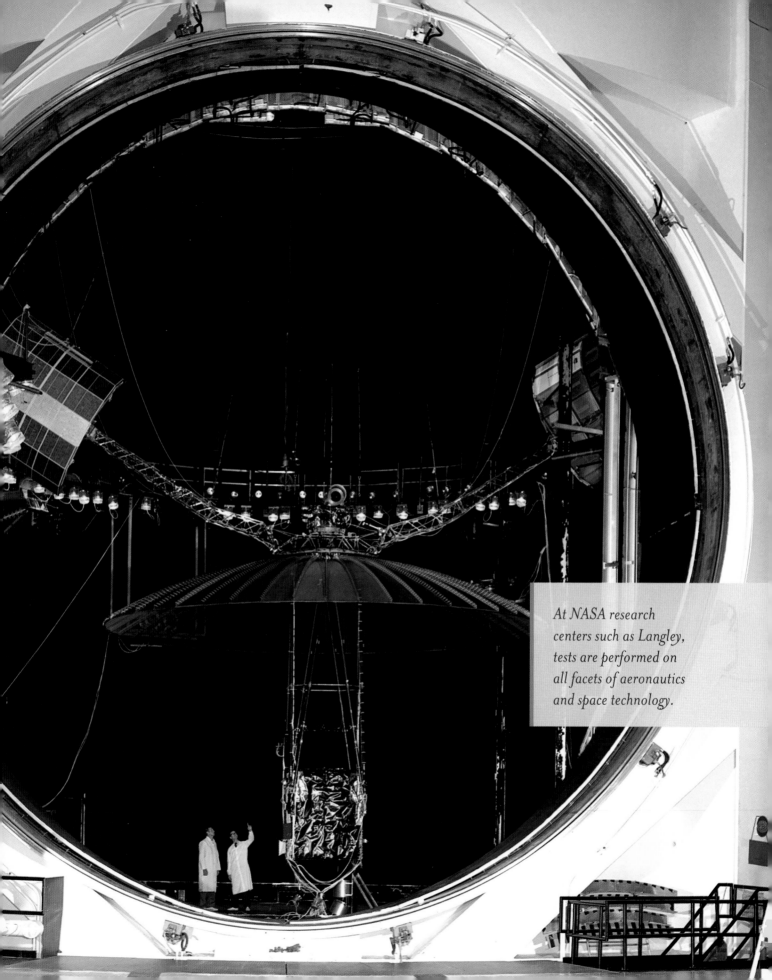

At NASA research centers such as Langley, tests are performed on all facets of aeronautics and space technology.

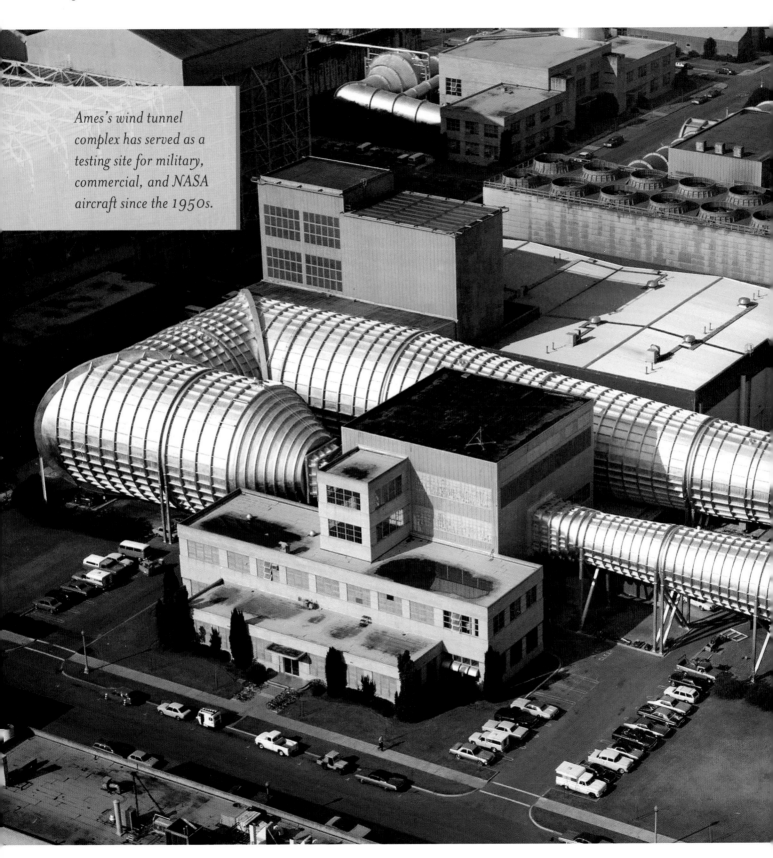

Ames's wind tunnel complex has served as a testing site for military, commercial, and NASA aircraft since the 1950s.

in Virginia, the Ames Aeronautical Laboratory in California, and the Lewis Flight Propulsion Laboratory (now Glenn Research Center) in Ohio. It also had NACA's Wallops Flight Facility in Virginia, a small test center for sounding rockets. In December 1958, NASA acquired the Jet Propulsion Laboratory in California. The following year, the Army Ballistic Missile Agency in Huntsville, Alabama, became NASA's fourth field center, the Marshall Space Flight Center. This was where the Saturn V rockets, which launched Apollo craft in the 1960s, were developed. Other field centers operated by NASA include the Armstrong Flight Research Center, the Goddard Space Flight Center, and the Stennis Space Center. Perhaps the two most prominent field centers, though, are Florida's Kennedy Space Center (the launch site for many shuttles, satellites, and other space vehicles) and the Johnson Space Center in Houston, Texas, the home of mission control.

As an independent federal agency, NASA receives funding from the federal government. NASA's original budget in 1958 was $100 million. Just 2 years later, however, NASA received $500 million in funds. Its budget ballooned to $5.2 billion in 1965 (4 percent of the overall federal budget), to fuel the Apollo program. In 2014, NASA's budget stood at $17.6 billion (0.5 percent of the overall federal budget). It spends most of its annual funds on the ISS and space transportation, exploration, and research and technology programs. In addition, the thousands of pieces of data and images collected by NASA over the years are easily accessible to anyone from anywhere in the world. NASA's human resources have also evolved with the changing times. In 1958, NASA consisted of 170 employees plus 8,000 former NACA employees. After hitting its peak of 411,000 in-house and outside contract employees in 1965, NASA gradually decreased staff until it ended up with about 18,000 in-house workers in 2013. Down from the hundreds of thousands of outside contractors hired during Project Apollo, the average number in recent years has settled around 60,000.

NASA employees represent a variety of

NASA's original budget in 1958 was $100 million.... In 2014, NASA's budget stood at $17.6 billion.

professions, including astronauts, scientists, engineers, artists, educators, information technology specialists, human resources specialists, accountants, writers, and technicians. Their diverse duties place them in laboratories, control rooms, classrooms, airfields, and beyond. NASA looks for people with backgrounds in medicine, microbiology, geology, physics, electrical engineering, and many other fields.

To prepare for a career as an astronaut, an individual must have a college degree in an applicable field such as in math, physics, astronomy, or chemistry. Before they can become astronauts, candidates must undergo two years of basic training. Most of this training takes place in the classroom, where candidates learn about vehicle and space station systems and study such subjects as earth science and engineering that will help them on missions. Candidates must also complete land and water survival training, where they prepare for an unplanned landing back on Earth, and must pass a swimming test.

After candidates complete basic training, they can be selected to become astronauts. Then astronaut trainees are paired with experienced astronauts, who share their launch, orbit, and landing skills. The final leg—advanced training—is a grueling 10-month period during

AGENCY INSIDER

VALENTINA TERESHKOVA

On June 16, 1963, Soviet cosmonaut Valentina Tereshkova became the first woman to travel into space when she made 48 orbits and logged 71 hours aboard Vostok 6. At that point, she had spent more time in space than all U.S. astronauts combined. The first American woman to travel into space, Sally Ride, made her historic flight on June 18, 1983, aboard the space shuttle *Challenger*. The *Challenger* exploded three years later.

Underwater training conditions on Earth help astronauts get a feel for the weightless environment of space.

which astronauts receive their mission and focus on specific activities, tools, and experiments they will need on their mission. Before the space shuttle program ended in 2011, most astronaut training was done at Johnson Space Center, but since then, many astronauts train at Star City, a cosmonaut training facility near Moscow.

Administrative positions are usually held by former astronauts or military officers or others with extensive knowledge of engineering and aviation. NASA's 12th administrator, Charles Bolden Jr., was nominated by president Barack Obama and confirmed by the U.S. Senate in 2009. Bolden spent 14 years out of a 34-year career with the Marine Corps as a member of NASA's Astronaut Office. Between 1986 and

1994, he traveled to space four times, piloting the mission that delivered the Hubble Space Telescope to orbit in 1990.

In his time at NASA, Bolden has helped the agency shift its focus from space shuttle missions to new explorations and technology. To that end, he has encouraged the development of new vehicles to transport astronauts to asteroids, Mars, and other places in deep space. In 2011, he helped establish the Space Technology Mission Directorate to ensure that future missions were equipped with state-of-the-art capabilities. Under Bolden's watch, NASA's accomplishments included the 2011 launch of the *Juno* spacecraft to Jupiter, the 2012 landing of the Curiosity **rover** on Mars, and continued work on the JWST.

About the size of a car, Curiosity was bound for the Martian Mount Sharp as its mission continued in 2014.

GPM CORE OBSERVATORY
Tanegashima, Japan

In February 2014, the launch of the Global Precipitation Measurement (GPM) Core Observatory from Japan's Tanegashima Space Center made headlines worldwide. In partnership with NASA, the Japan Aerospace Exploration Agency (JAXA) sought to establish new standards for making observations of rain and snow from space. GPM data will contribute to climate research and the forecasting of extreme natural disasters such as floods and hurricanes. Scientists also hope to use GPM to study Earth's water and energy cycles.

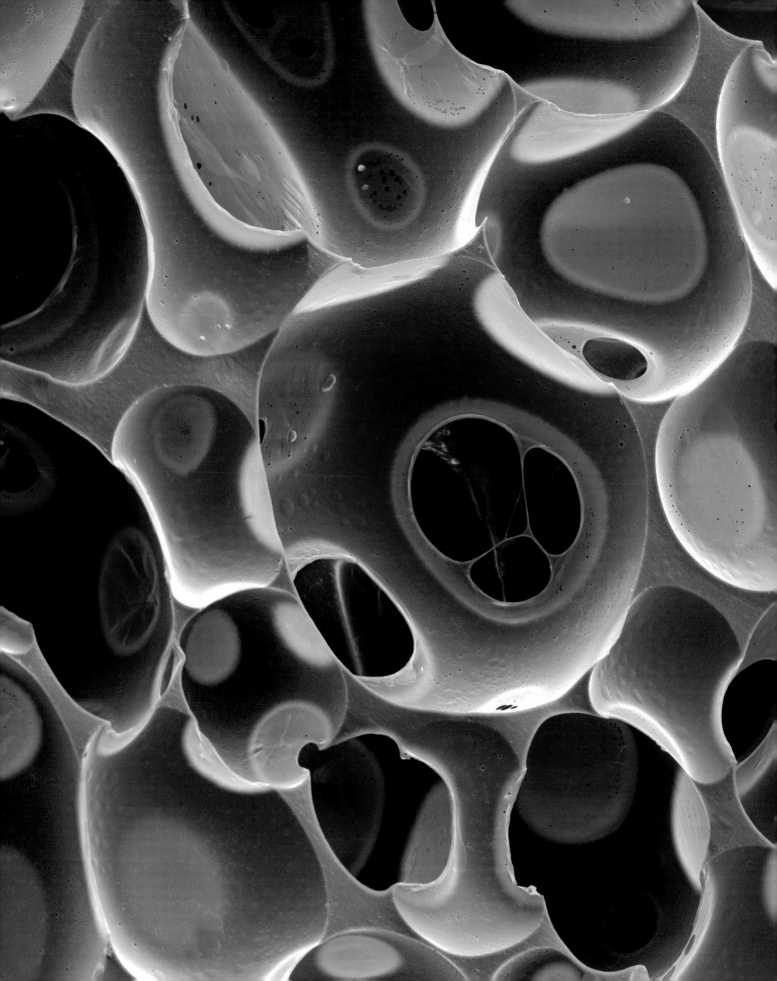

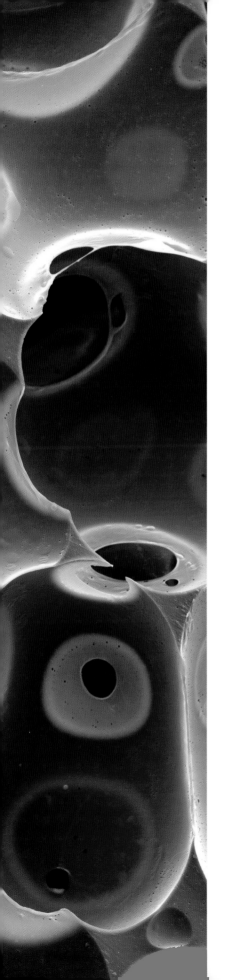

A New Space Age

Throughout the last six decades, NASA has achieved many technological breakthroughs and faced many challenges. Although most people today will never set foot on the moon, they likely encounter—or use—a NASA invention every day. Partnering with various research teams and companies, NASA continues to spawn new technologies and products that have improved our daily lives. Important steps in health, safety, communications, and even entertainment find their roots in the government branch associated with rocket ships and floating people. Common household products invented by NASA include memory foam for mattresses, scratch-resistant eyeglass lenses, ear thermometers, handheld vacuum cleaners, and water filters.

Significant medical breakthroughs can also be attributed to NASA. In 1995, Dr. Michael DeBakey of the Baylor College of Medicine teamed up with Johnson Space Center engineer David Saucier to develop an artificial heart pump. Based on the design of the main engine fuel pumps in space shuttles, the heart pump was able to help people who were waiting for

The stretchy nature of memory foam—commercially available since 1991—can be seen on a microscopic level.

heart transplants keep blood pumping through their bodies. In the 1960s, Pillsbury Company invented a system for NASA—called the Hazard Analysis and Critical Control Point system—to ensure that the astronauts on the way to the moon would not get food poisoning. Thirty years later, the U.S. Food and Drug Administration and the Department of Agriculture adopted these standards nationwide, which resulted in a 20 percent reduction in food-borne illness and lower medical costs.

Beginning in the 1960s, satellites launched by NASA revolutionized the meteorology, global communications, and navigation industries. The seven Nimbus satellites, which went up in the 1960s and '70s, carried advanced television cloud-mapping cameras and **infrared radiometers** that allowed photos of weather fronts and storms to be taken at night for the first time. In 1984, *Nimbus 7* revealed the first evidence of a hole in the **ozone** over Antarctica. Scientists tracked this phenomenon for the next few years as ozone levels continued to decrease. This discovery led to a 1987 ban on chemicals that depleted the ozone layer.

NASA made global communications a reality when it cooperated with AT&T to send *Telstar 1* into orbit in 1962. *Telstar* was designed to receive signals from Earth-based antennae and relay them to stations elsewhere on the ground. On July 12, 1962, a giant, movable antenna near Andover, Maine, locked onto the satellite when its shifting orbit reached a certain point. Minutes later, the first television pictures were transmitted across the Atlantic Ocean and received on European television screens. Telephone, telegraph, data, telephoto, and facsimile transmissions were also successfully made. With that, the age of electronic communications had begun.

In the 1970s, a major breakthrough came with the development of the global positioning system (GPS). GPS is a space-based satellite navigation system that provides location and time data in all weather conditions. Developed by the U.S. Department of Defense, it can operate anywhere on or near Earth where there is an unobstructed line of sight to four or more GPS satellites. (Today, there are 24 satellites used for GPS.) The system is maintained by the U.S. government but is freely accessible to anyone with a GPS receiver.

> *... in the 1960s, satellites launched by NASA revolutionized the meteorology, global communications, and navigation industries.*

Non-GPS satellites such as Terra collect valuable data about Earth by capturing images rather than sending signals.

Prior to the planned 2017 launch of the SLS, artists were tasked with visualizing what such a scene would look like.

Spurred by the success of GPS, other nations have developed their own global satellite systems, including the Russian Global Navigation Satellite System (GLONASS), the European Union's Galileo positioning system, and China's Beidou satellite navigation system.

Wherever NASA gained technological progress, though, there were always critics and unforeseen consequences. After only 6 years in orbit (rather than the projected 8 to 10), Skylab fell back to Earth in 1979. Pieces of it were found from the southeastern part of the Indian Ocean to western Australia. People suddenly realized the dangers that falling space objects presented. Many were also concerned that potentially harmful chemicals in the debris would find their way into people's homes and backyards. As a result of the incident, NASA officials put greater safety measures in place to prevent such accidents from happening. No matter how careful NASA is, though, space exploration and travel are complicated and often dangerous, and other accidents will likely occur.

In the future, NASA will face many challenges in maintaining its level of technological achievement. During much of the early 2000s, the U.S. concentrated most of its federal budget on fighting wars in Iraq and Afghanistan. Then, in 2010, President Obama created a new space policy that called for a focus on technology improvements rather than human exploration. As a result, the underfunded Constellation program (which aimed to send Americans back to the moon and eventually Mars) was cancelled. NASA then looked for other ways to explore, mostly through partnerships. The Inspiration Mars Foundation, led by multimillionaire Dennis Tito, is a planned partnership with NASA to send a man and a woman on a flyby mission to Mars in 2018. If it succeeds, Inspiration Mars would be the first manned spaceflight to the Red Planet.

All of NASA's 10 field centers became involved in a new venture with private aircraft company Boeing and other partners in 2014. Researching, testing, and building were underway on the Space Launch System (SLS), the successor to the shuttle. Using powerful rocket boosters, the SLS will be able to explore deep-space destinations such as the moon,

Wherever NASA gained technological progress, though, there were always critics and unforeseen consequences.

asteroids, and Mars. The crew vehicle for the SLS, *Orion*, was also in development by NASA and global security and aerospace company Lockheed Martin. *Orion* will be NASA's first spacecraft to feature a launch abort system— a way for the crew to escape should anything go wrong at launch. In December 2014, *Orion* completed a test flight to help researchers evaluate several important systems. *Orion*'s planned flight path into deep space will expose astronauts to much higher levels of radiation than past space missions. This will require developing new technologies to keep astronauts safe.

Amidst progress on the SLS, NASA also committed resources to other related endeavors, such as its "Asteroid Initiative." In 2013, NASA announced plans to launch a robotic spacecraft toward a 500-ton (454 t) asteroid that would pull it to a stable orbit near the moon. Relocating the asteroid would reduce the amount of time it would take astronauts to reach the asteroid to study it. Astronauts planned to learn how to prevent asteroids from crashing into Earth— such as the asteroid that exploded over Russia in February 2013, injuring more than 1,000 people. However, some questioned the need to fund the $100-million asteroid mission at all. Instead,

AGENCY INSIDER

APOLLO 1

Project Apollo did not begin well. On January 27, 1967, a flash fire engulfed the Apollo 1 command module during a launch pad test, trapping and killing all three astronauts inside. Although the source of the fire could not be found, several design and construction flaws were identified. In response, NASA removed flammable items from the module and redesigned the hatch door so that it would open instantly when the crew needed to exit.

One of Orion's tests involved the system responsible for flipping the vehicle right-side up, in case landing went awry.

they wanted the U.S. to join forces with other countries to conduct a comprehensive survey of all potentially dangerous asteroids.

In 2013, NASA selected proposals from 250 U.S. small businesses and 25 research institutions to help fund its future missions. The proposals are part of NASA's Small Business Innovation Research Program (SBIR) and Small Business Technology Transfer (STTR) Program. Such partnerships will be critical to NASA's continuing space missions, including those involving the ISS. Administrator Bolden said private companies were expected to launch astronauts to the orbiting platform beginning in 2017.

NASA also looked to expand its cooperative efforts with other nations. The JWST is an international collaboration among NASA, the ESA, and the Canadian Space Agency. When it launches in 2018, it is likely to help thousands of astronomers around the world study the universe. Scientists are planning to use the $8-billion infrared telescope to take photos, search for the universe's first galaxies, and look for signs of where and how the solar system began.

In NASA's more than 50 years as the country's leader in aeronautics, it has led the movement from a focus on lunar landing to space shuttle missions to ISS exploration and the development of deep-space and aeronautics technology. Armed with 21st-century technology, international support, and the capability of exploring the far reaches of the universe, NASA continues to push the boundaries of what is possible—or, in the words of the Armstrong Flight Research Center's vision statement, "to fly what others only imagine."

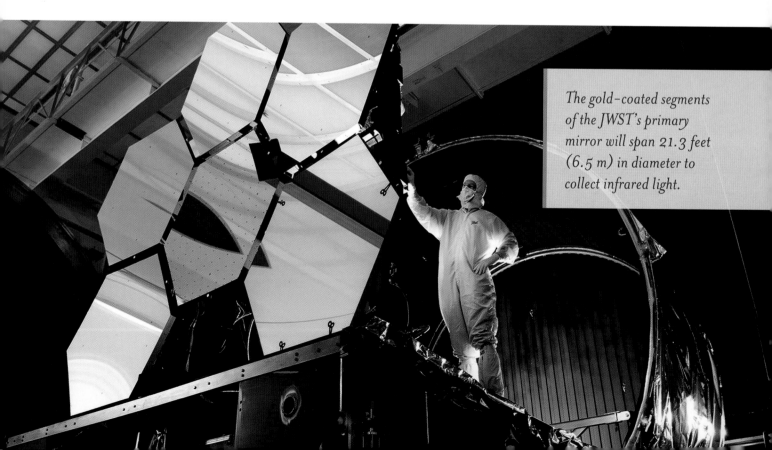

The gold-coated segments of the JWST's primary mirror will span 21.3 feet (6.5 m) in diameter to collect infrared light.

"EARTHRISE"
Moon

The first manned mission to lunar orbit, Apollo 8, launched on December 21, 1968. It carried astronauts Frank Borman, James Lovell, and William Anders. The first humans to see Earth from the moon's orbit, the crew took spectacular photos of Earth above the moon's horizon, including one later known as "Earthrise." Called one of the most influential photographs ever taken, it allowed people to see Earth as a fragile object and marked the beginning of the environmental movement.

GLOSSARY

aeronautical relating to the science or practice of all aspects of flight through the air

airfoil a structure on an aircraft, such as a wing, propeller blade, or rudder, that is shaped to lift the aircraft into the air

aviation the design, development, production, operation, and use of aircraft

celestial relating to the sky, or space beyond Earth's atmosphere

Cold War a period of rivalry after World War II between the communist Soviet Union and the democratic United States

counterculture a way of life at odds with the larger culture, or society, at the time

cowling the removable cover of a vehicle or aircraft engine

Earth orbit a path around Earth followed by an object in space

infrared radiometers devices that measure the power of radiation from radio waves, infrared, visible light, ultraviolet, X-rays, and gamma rays

microgravity a condition of very weak gravity, resulting in weightlessness

module an independent, self-contained segment of a spacecraft that is designed to break away from other units

nuclear powered by energy made by the fusing or splitting of atoms

O-rings shaped pieces of rubber used to seal together interlocking pipes or tubes

ozone a gas that forms a layer in Earth's atmosphere and absorbs most of the sun's ultraviolet light

payload the people and equipment carried by a spacecraft

radiation characterized by energy given off by highly charged particles

reconnaissance related to information gathering or scouting

rover a remote-control vehicle used to gather data on other planets

SELECTED BIBLIOGRAPHY

Dick, Steven, Robert Jacobs, Constance Moore, and Bertram Ulrich. *America in Space: NASA's First Fifty Years*. New York: Abrams, 2007.

Furniss, Tim. *A History of Space Exploration and Its Future*. Guilford, Conn.: Lyons Press, 2003.

Gorn, Michael H. *NASA: The Complete Illustrated History*. New York: Merrell, 2005.

Krige, John, Angelina Long Callahan, and Ashok Maharaj. *NASA in the World: Fifty Years of International Collaboration in Space*. New York: Palgrave Macmillan, 2013.

Launius, Roger D. *NASA: A History of the U.S. Civil Space Program*. Malabar, Fla.: Krieger, 1994.

Launius, Roger D., and Bertram Ulrich. *NASA & the Exploration of Space*. New York: Stewart, Tabori & Chang, 1998.

National Aeronautics and Space Administration. "Homepage." http://www.nasa.gov/.

Space.com. "Homepage." http://www.space.com/.

WEBSITES

NASA's Eyes on the Solar System
http://eyes.nasa.gov/index.html
Fly with NASA's *Voyager*, control space and time, or even hop on an asteroid, all from the comfort of your own home.

NASA's The Space Place
http://spaceplace.nasa.gov/menu/explore/
Explore the sun, Earth, and the rest of our solar system, and learn more about space technology.

Note: Every effort has been made to ensure that the websites listed above are suitable for children, that they have educational value, and that they contain no inappropriate material. However, because of the nature of the Internet, it is impossible to guarantee that these sites will remain active indefinitely or that their contents will not be altered.

INDEX